# MAKING CRAZY ANIMALS

*Design*      David West
                  Children's Book Design
*Designer*   Keith Newell
*Editor*      Michael Flaherty
*Photography*  Roger Vlitos

© Aladdin Books 1992

First published in
the United States in 1992 by
Gloucester Press Inc
95 Madison Ave
New York, NY 10016

Library of Congress Cataloging-in-Publication Data

Green, Jen M.
    Making crazy animals / by Jen Green.
      p.    cm. — (Why throw it away?)
    Includes index.
    Summary: Presents step-by-step instructions for making pigs,
tortoises, snakes and other papier-mâché animals using
simple techniques and materials.
    ISBN 0-531-17324-0
    1. Papier-mâché—Juvenile literature. 2. Animals in art—
Juvenile literature. [1. Papier-mâché. 2. Animals in art.
3. Handicraft.] I. Title. II. Series.
TT871.R62    1992
745.592—dc20      91-33868    CIP    AC

Printed in Belgium

# Why throw it away?

# MAKING CRAZY ANIMALS

## JEN GREEN

GLOUCESTER PRESS
New York: London: Toronto: Sydney

# CONTENTS

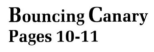

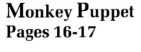

# INTRODUCTION

This book will show you how to create your own collection of crazy animals. Each of the projects is explained in easy stages. There are also more ideas about how you can adapt the models, bringing in your own imagination.

### Anything goes

All the models shown here can be made with everyday junk that you and your family usually throw away. Each project includes a list of junk items that can be used to make the model. But if you haven't got one of the items suggested, don't worry; you may have something else that will do just as well.

### Your junk collection

Start your own collection of junk materials now. Save any materials that might come in useful, and ask your family to pass on junk to you rather than throw it away. Make sure your materials are clean before you store them in plastic bags or in a big cardboard box. For more ideas about the kinds of junk you can collect, see page 29. There are also patterns and practical hints at the end of the book.

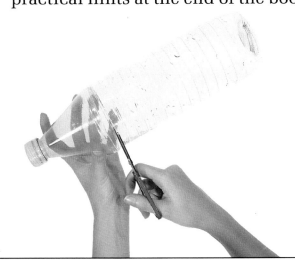

# Crazy Animal Heads

These colorful animal heads are all made from odds and ends of junk stuck onto a cardboard base such as a paper plate. You can use the same methods with different ingredients to make your own animal heads.

## Step By Step

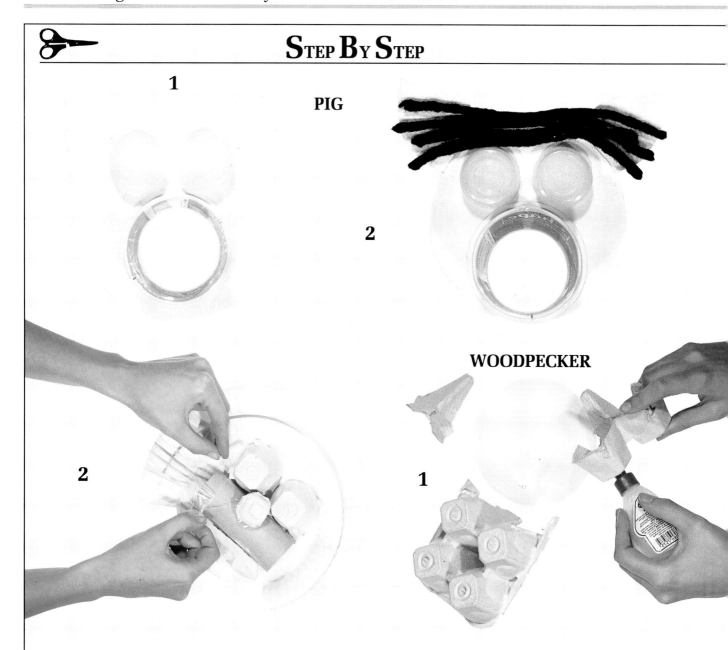

**1**

**PIG**

**2**

**WOODPECKER**

**2**

**1**

**To make the pig:**
**1** You will need two bottle tops for eyes, a plastic cup for the nose, yarn, ear shapes cut from cardboard, and a cardboard circle for the head. You could make the circle by cutting the rim off a paper plate. **2** Tape or glue on the bottle tops to make the eyes and the cup for the nose. Glue on yarn for the hair.

**To make the lion:**
**1** You will need two sections cut from an egg carton for the eyes, a toilet paper tube for the muzzle, toothpicks for whiskers, and two paper plates with part of the rims cut away. **2** Glue one plate inside the other to make the mane. Cut the toilet tube in half to make a muzzle. Add egg carton eyes, nose and teeth. Lastly, tape on toothpick whiskers.

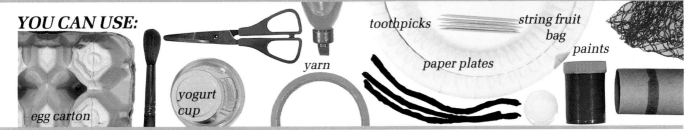

toothpicks   string fruit bag

yarn   paper plates   paints

yogurt cup

egg carton

---

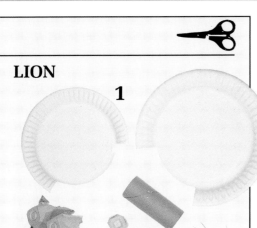

**LION**

**1**

**2**

**To make the woodpecker:**
**1** You will need a string fruit bag, a circle of cardboard and sections cut from an egg carton as shown. Glue on the egg carton eyes and the point for the beak. **2** Glue on the string bag for the woodpecker's topknot.

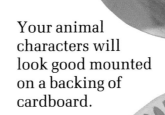

Your animal characters will look good mounted on a backing of cardboard.

Odds and ends at home may suggest other animals to try. A cow would need a black and white face, and cardboard horns. A donkey needs a long nose and ears, and a pink tongue.

To make the eyes, you could use cotton balls, or a Ping Pong ball cut in half.

When your models are complete and the glue has dried, color the heads using bright poster paint (see page 28 for tips on paint). Place the models on a sheet of newspaper first, as painting can be messy.

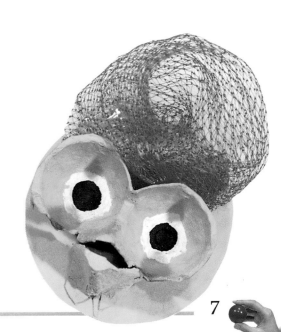

7

# FARMYARD MOBILE

This mobile will look spectacular hung from a shelf or lampshade, where it can spin freely. Using your imagination, you can adapt these egg carton designs to make other zoo and farmyard animals.

---

## STEP BY STEP

1 The bodies of the bee and pig are made from segments cut from an egg carton and taped together. 2 Cut the bee's wings from foil and tape them on. 3 To make the pig's snout, make a small hole in the end of the body. Insert the top of a dishwashing liquid bottle. 4 Pigs can sometimes fly. Cardboard wings have been taped to this one, and a wire tail is added. 5 Tape a long thread to the back of both animals. 6 The daffodils are made from tissue paper, straws and segments of candy box tray. 7 Cut the tissue paper into petal shapes.

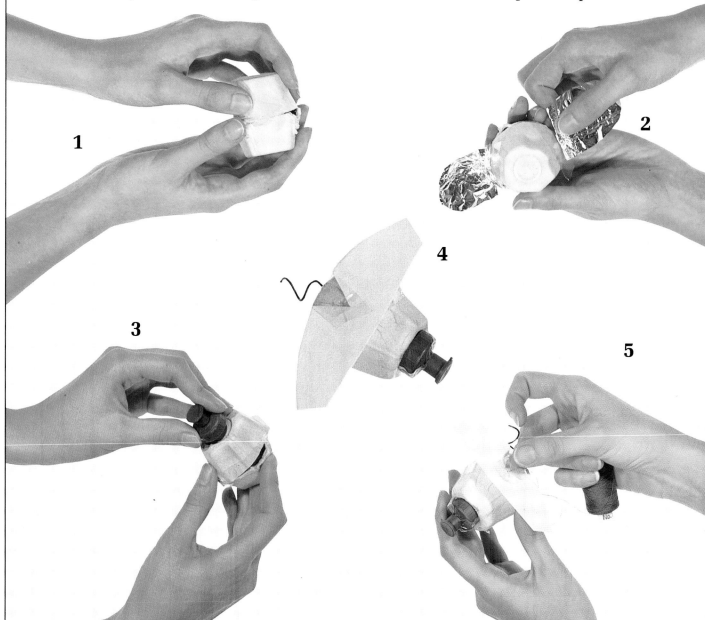

**YOU CAN USE:**

foil

drinking straws

egg carton

thread

candy box tray

Glue on straw stems and candy tray trumpets. **8** Bind two short pieces of garden stick with string, to form a cross. String the flowers and the animals from it. If the mobile isn't balanced, add modeling clay blobs to the models to even it up.

You can use a large paper clip to hook the model onto a shelf. You could also hang it on a string, so it can turn freely.

**6**

**7**

**8**

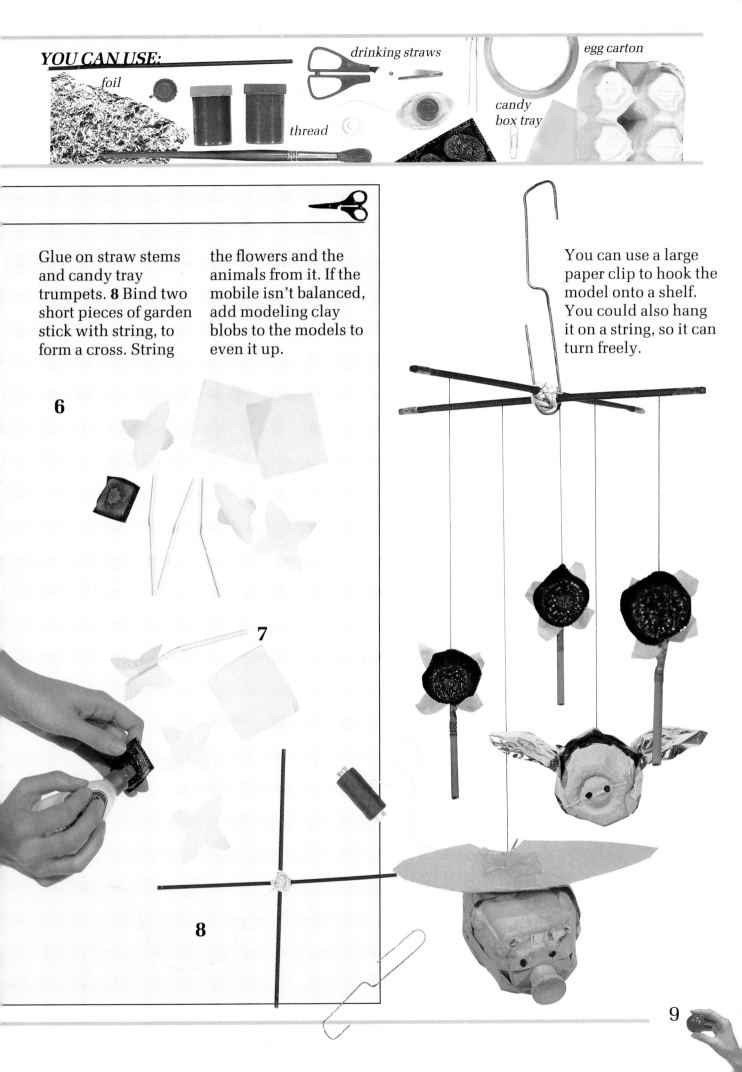

9

# BOUNCING CANARY

The canary is easy to make and will bounce merrily from a window or bookshelf, flapping its wings. Its secret is an egg carton body weighted with modeling clay. You can adapt this design to make a spider or seagull.

## ✂ STEP BY STEP

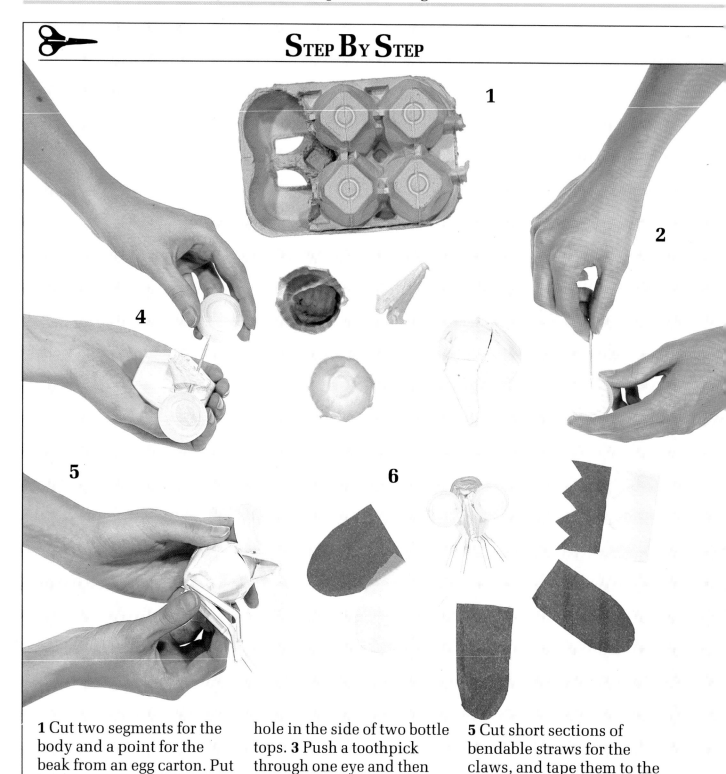

1 Cut two segments for the body and a point for the beak from an egg carton. Put modeling clay inside the body and tape it all together.
2 To make the eyes, pierce a hole in the side of two bottle tops. 3 Push a toothpick through one eye and then through the beak.
4 Push the other eye onto the end of the toothpick.

5 Cut short sections of bendable straws for the claws, and tape them to the body. 6 Cut paper shapes for the wings, tail and topknot.
7 Now tape on the wings,

**YOU CAN USE:** *plastic bottle tops*

*rubber bands*

*toothpick*

*straws*

*tissue paper*

*egg carton*

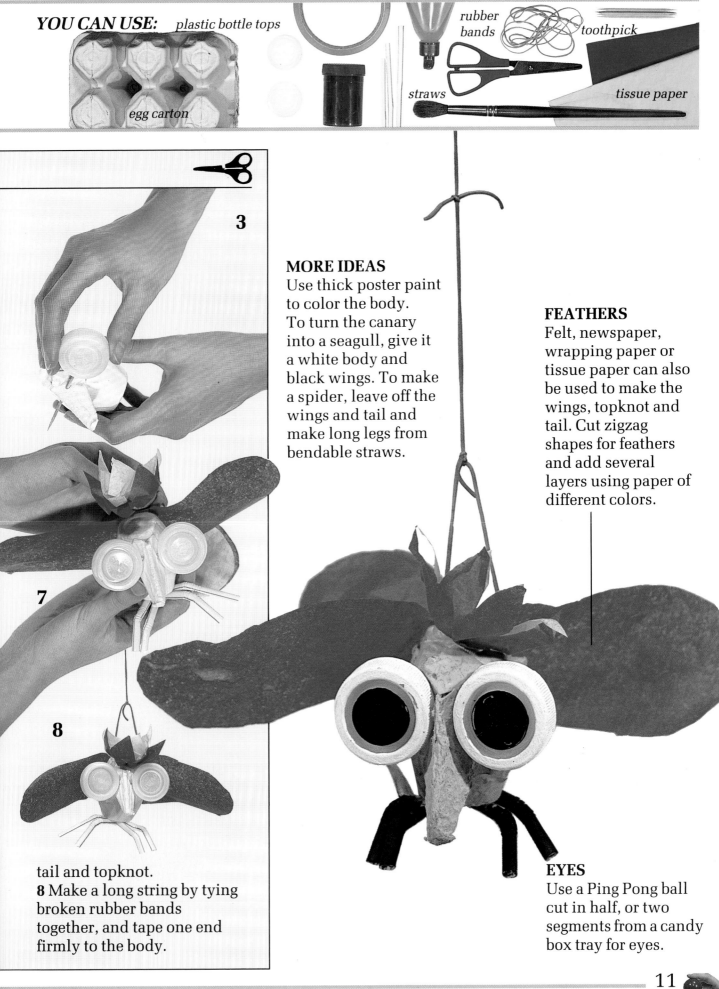

**3**

**MORE IDEAS**
Use thick poster paint to color the body. To turn the canary into a seagull, give it a white body and black wings. To make a spider, leave off the wings and tail and make long legs from bendable straws.

**FEATHERS**
Felt, newspaper, wrapping paper or tissue paper can also be used to make the wings, topknot and tail. Cut zigzag shapes for feathers and add several layers using paper of different colors.

**7**

**8**

tail and topknot.
**8** Make a long string by tying broken rubber bands together, and tape one end firmly to the body.

**EYES**
Use a Ping Pong ball cut in half, or two segments from a candy box tray for eyes.

11

# SLITHERY SNAKE

This colorful snake has a wriggly body made of yogurt cups. It will sway and twist in your hand in a lifelike manner. You could alter this design to make either a caterpillar or a crocodile.

**1** The body of the slithery snake is made of seven or eight plastic cups. Make sure the pots are clean before you use them. With a toothpick, pierce holes on opposite sides of the pots at the top and the base.

Hold the base of one cup just inside the top of another cup and line up the holes. Pass a toothpick through the holes so that one cup hangs inside the other.

Repeat this step with the other cups until you have built the snake's body of seven or eight sections.

**2** Cut a forked tongue from tissue paper and add it to one end of the body as shown to make the head.

**3** Cut eyes from sections of an egg carton and tape them to the head of your snake.

**4** Stick the tops of two cups together to form a tail at the other end of the body.

**5** Your slithery snake is now ready for you to paint and decorate it. Color your snake with thick poster paint. To make the paint stick to plastic, follow the practical tip on page 28. Add stripes or spots to decorate the body. Paint dark V-shapes on the head and body to turn your snake into a viper.

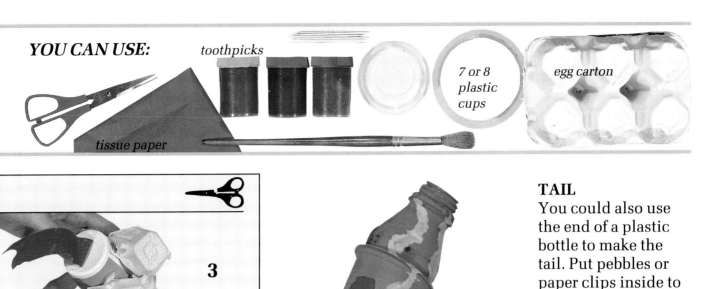
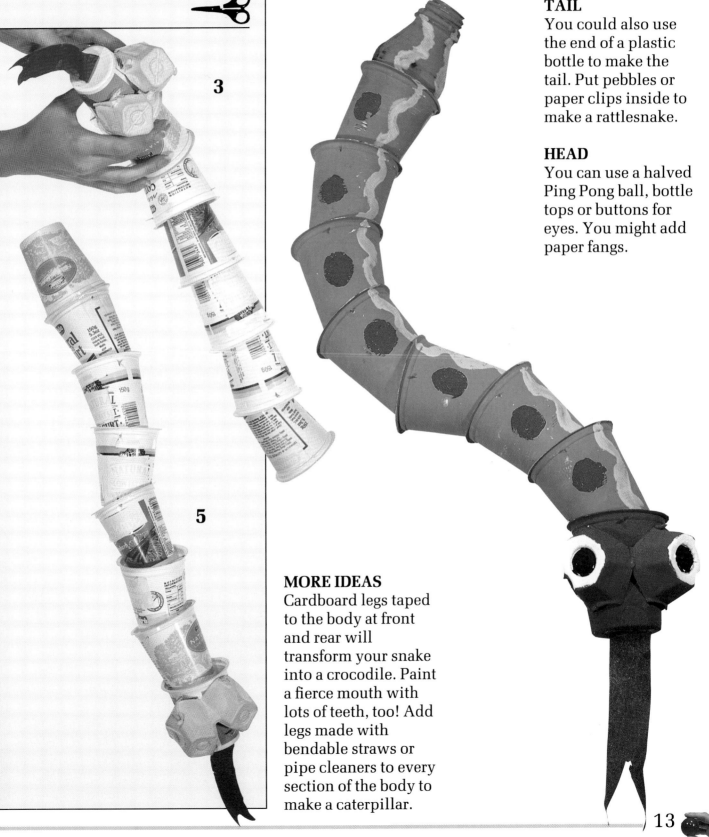

**3**

**5**

### TAIL
You could also use the end of a plastic bottle to make the tail. Put pebbles or paper clips inside to make a rattlesnake.

### HEAD
You can use a halved Ping Pong ball, bottle tops or buttons for eyes. You might add paper fangs.

### MORE IDEAS
Cardboard legs taped to the body at front and rear will transform your snake into a crocodile. Paint a fierce mouth with lots of teeth, too! Add legs made with bendable straws or pipe cleaners to every section of the body to make a caterpillar.

# NODDING BEAGLE

The nodding beagle has a head that rocks on a garden stick pivot. It will nod soulfully, from the back window of your family's car, perhaps. You can alter this design to make a rabbit instead.

This beagle's shaggy fringe is cut from the edge of a paper plate. You could glue on strands of yarn instead.

When the model is complete, color it with poster paint. Your beagle could be black or white with spots or patches, or you could choose a different breed.

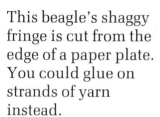

**1**

You could make a kennel for your beagle out of a clean milk carton or small box. Cut a doorway in one side to fit your model.

You can alter this design to make many different animals. For example, by adding long cardboard ears and a fluffy tail of cotton balls you can turn this model into a rabbit.

**1** Cut out the middle section of a plastic bottle. Cut it again as shown, leaving two tabs to form the neck pivot. Pierce a hole through the center of each tab. **2** The beagle's head is a plastic cup

# STEP BY STEP

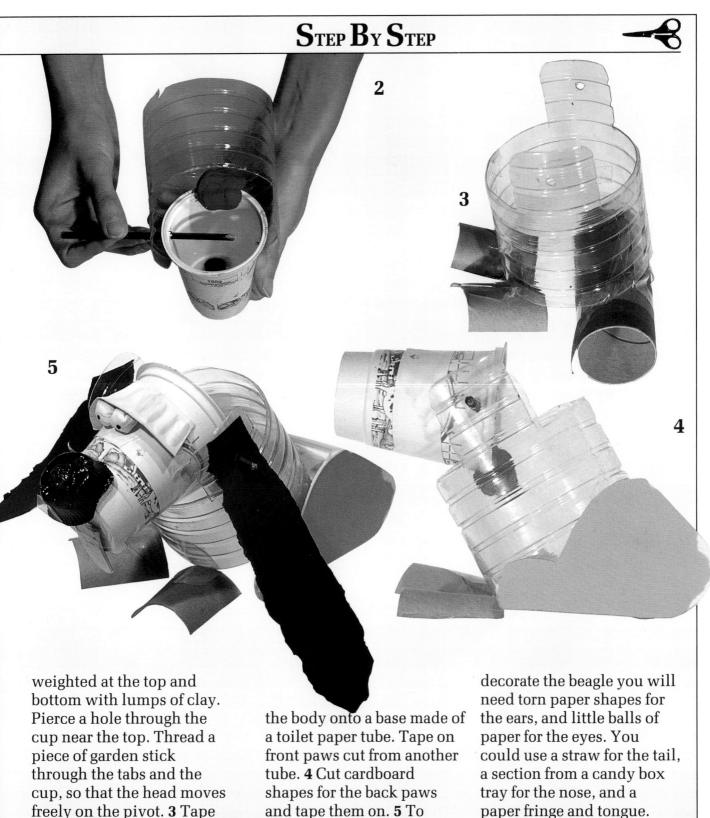

2

3

5

4

weighted at the top and bottom with lumps of clay. Pierce a hole through the cup near the top. Thread a piece of garden stick through the tabs and the cup, so that the head moves freely on the pivot. **3** Tape the body onto a base made of a toilet paper tube. Tape on front paws cut from another tube. **4** Cut cardboard shapes for the back paws and tape them on. **5** To decorate the beagle you will need torn paper shapes for the ears, and little balls of paper for the eyes. You could use a straw for the tail, a section from a candy box tray for the nose, and a paper fringe and tongue.

15

# Monkey Puppet

This monkey is a marionette, or string puppet. It is easy to make and great fun to operate. This design can be altered to make an elephant, and many other animals – the choice is yours!

## Step By Step

**1** Tape a small cardboard box to a larger one to make the head and body. **2** Cut eyes from an egg carton. **3** Cut a large and a small circle of cardboard. Cut the circles in half. **4** Tape a strip of colored tissue between the halves of the smaller circle, to make the muzzle. **5** Cut two long thin strips of paper for the arms, and shorter, wider ones for the legs. Crease the paper into accordion folds and add

## YOU CAN USE:

paper disks
or plates

yarn

straws

box

cardboard box

egg carton

**4**

**7**

straws for fingers and toes.
**6** Tape onto the head the
eyes, muzzle, and the halves
of the larger circle to form
the ears. Tape the arms and
legs onto the body. Glue on a
paper plate for the tummy.
**7** Decorate your monkey
with yarn hair.

Paint your puppet
with poster paint.
You could add a tail
of paper with
accordion folds, and a
hat made from a
plastic cup.

This design can be
altered to make many
other animals. You
could make an
elephant, with a long
trunk made of plastic
cups linked with
toothpicks (see pages
12-13). Paint the
elephant gray with
pink toenails.

**17**

# STRINGING THE MONKEY PUPPET

Complete your monkey marionette by stringing it to a frame. You could team up with a friend and make other animal puppets. Invent an adventure for the puppets, and then put on a performance for your family and friends.

## STEP BY STEP

**1** To string your puppet you will need two short pieces of garden stake, and four lengths of string: a long piece for the body, two medium lengths for the arms, and a short piece for the head. Make the frame by binding the sticks into a cross with string. Tie the strings to the frame. Attach the arm strings to opposite points of the cross, and tie the short head string to the middle. **2** Tape the arm strings firmly to the puppet's wrists. **3** Tape the body string to the base of the back. **4** Tape on the head string.

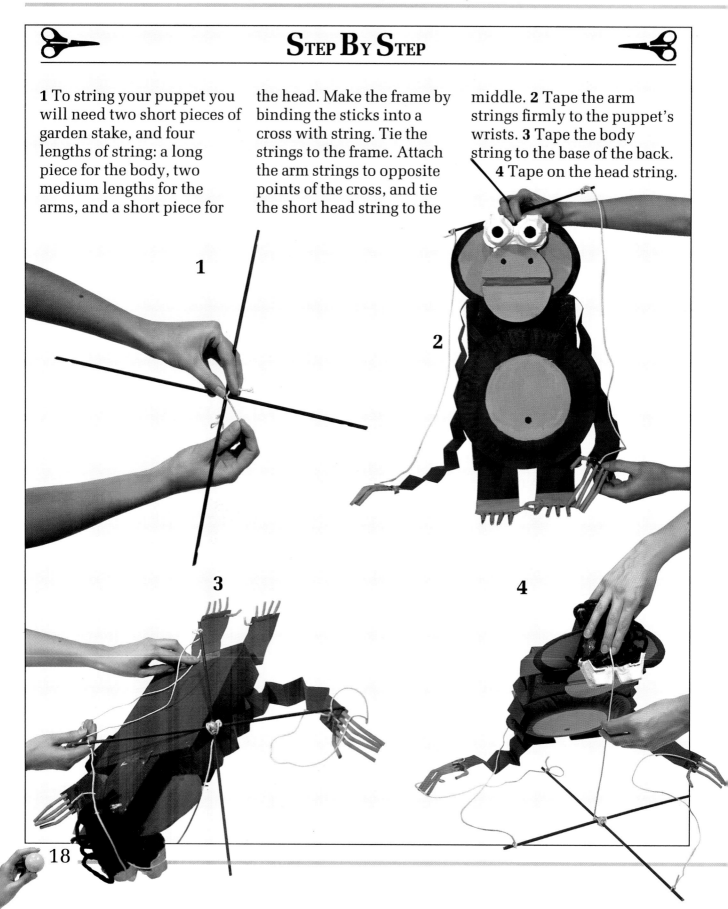

cotton thread
or string

sticks or garden stakes

tape

scissors

Tilt the frame to one side, or lift the arm strings one at a time to make the puppet wave or beckon. Tilt the frame from side to side to give it a swaggering walking movement. Dip the front of the frame in order to make your puppet bow.

Practice moving the crossframe to make your puppet jump and dance.

19

# Tortoise Bank

The shell of this tortoise is made from papier mâché, a term which comes from the French words for mashed paper. Papier mâché can be messy, so wear old clothes and cover your work surface with newspaper.

 **Step By Step**

**1** In a bowl, mix flour and water to make a thick paste. **2** Blow up a balloon and stand it in a bowl. Tear a newspaper into strips, and dip a strip in the paste. Run

the strip through your fingers to remove excess paste. Lay the strip over the balloon. Continue until the top half of the balloon is covered with at least three layers of newspaper.

**3** Leave the papier mâché shell until it is dry. Burst the balloon. Trim the bottom flat with scissors, and make a slit in the top. **4** Cut short slits in the neck

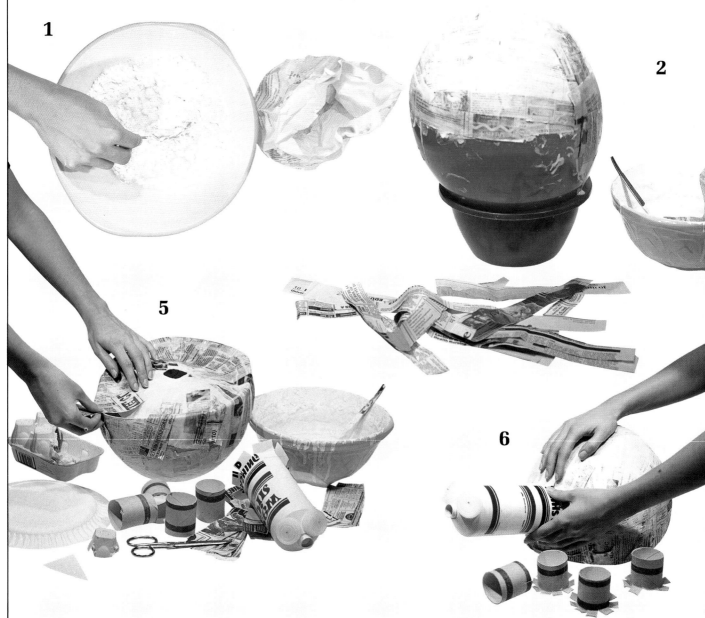

**YOU CAN USE:**

two toilet
paper tubes

modeling
clay

balloon

egg carton

flour

paper plate

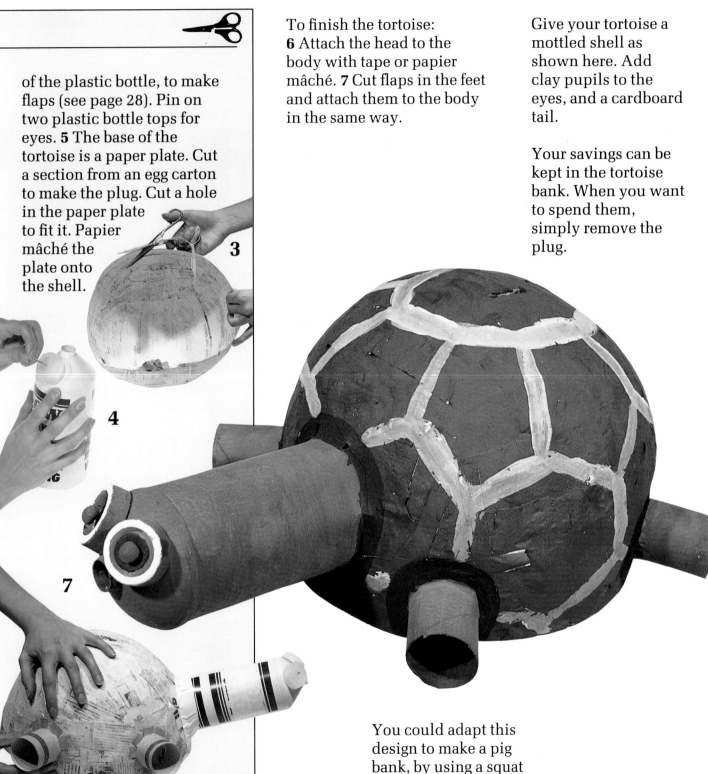

of the plastic bottle, to make flaps (see page 28). Pin on two plastic bottle tops for eyes. **5** The base of the tortoise is a paper plate. Cut a section from an egg carton to make the plug. Cut a hole in the paper plate to fit it. Papier mâché the plate onto the shell.

**3**

**4**

**7**

To finish the tortoise:
**6** Attach the head to the body with tape or papier mâché. **7** Cut flaps in the feet and attach them to the body in the same way.

Give your tortoise a mottled shell as shown here. Add clay pupils to the eyes, and a cardboard tail.

Your savings can be kept in the tortoise bank. When you want to spend them, simply remove the plug.

You could adapt this design to make a pig bank, by using a squat plastic cup for the nose. Add floppy cardboard ears, too.

# SHAPELY SWAN

This graceful bird is a simple project which uses only newspaper and cardboard to construct a sturdy frame. You can use the same design to make a Canada goose or a farmyard duck.

---

## STEP BY STEP

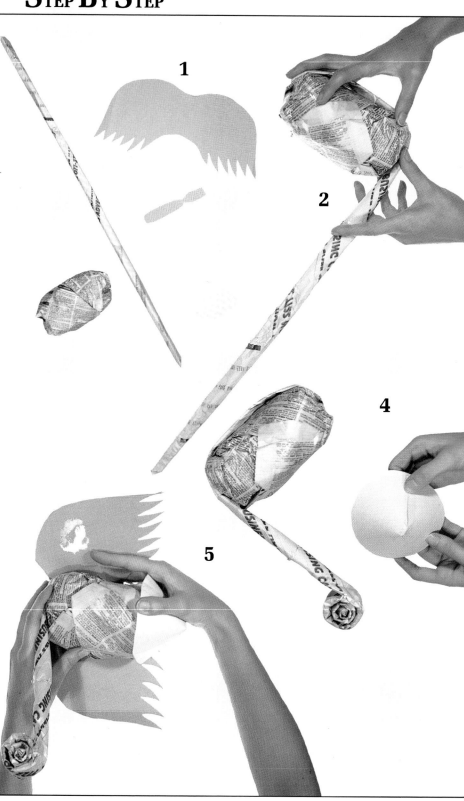

**1** To make the swan's body, you will need to scrunch several sheets of newspaper into a large, tight ball, and tape it together. Tape up another sheet into a long, tight roll. You will also need two small paper disks, a larger paper circle with a quarter section cut out, and a thin cardboard strip cut as shown. Cut cardboard wings using the help of the pattern on pages 30-31.

**2** Flatten and tape one end of the newspaper roll under the body and at the base of the neck. **3** Wind the other end of the roll around a pencil to create a tight curl. Tape it tightly together.

**4** Take the large paper disk with the quarter section removed and tape the sides together to make a cone. Then tape the cone to the body to make the tail.

**5** Hold the wings under the body. Crease them up around the body and tape them on. **6** Draw eyes on the two paper circles and glue or tape them to the head. To make the beak, fold the thin strip of cardboard you cut earlier. The fold is trimmed to form the point of the beak. Run the ends of the strip around either side of the head and tape them in place.

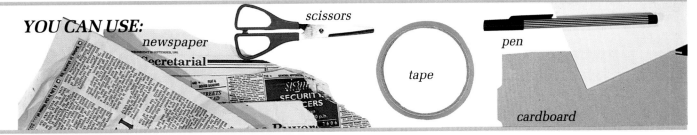

newspaper

scissors

tape

pen

cardboard

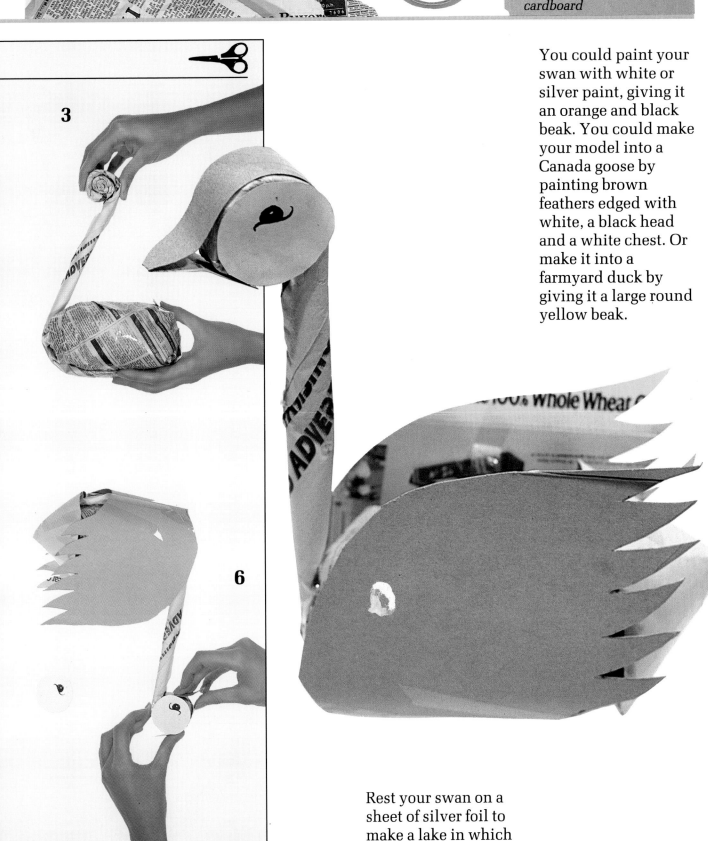

**3**

**6**

You could paint your swan with white or silver paint, giving it an orange and black beak. You could make your model into a Canada goose by painting brown feathers edged with white, a black head and a white chest. Or make it into a farmyard duck by giving it a large round yellow beak.

Rest your swan on a sheet of silver foil to make a lake in which it will be reflected.

# CRANKY CAMEL

This lordly animal is made by laying papier mâché over a newspaper frame, using the techniques you used to make the swan and tortoise. The camel is decorated with a paper saddle, and you can also add reins.

**1** Tightly roll up three sheets of newspaper. Tape them so they don't unfurl. Scrunch up three newspaper balls, and a smaller ball. Tape them up in the same way. Make a frame for the body by folding two long rolls over the third. You could secure them in position with tape. If the ends of the legs are uneven, even them up with scissors.

**2** Bend the neck up and tape the end tightly around the small newspaper ball to make the camel's head.

**3** Tape the three balls to the back to make the hump.

**4** Tear a newspaper into strips. Prepare a flour and water paste for papier mâché, as you did to make the tortoise bank (see pages 20-1). Cover the whole frame with at least three layers of newspaper strips. Support the model by looping and tying string around the legs. Leave it to dry overnight. Your camel is now ready for you to paint and decorate it.

**5** To make the saddle, decorate a rectangle of paper with paints or crayons. Cut four slits in it to fit over your camel's hump. Fold and tape it around the hump.

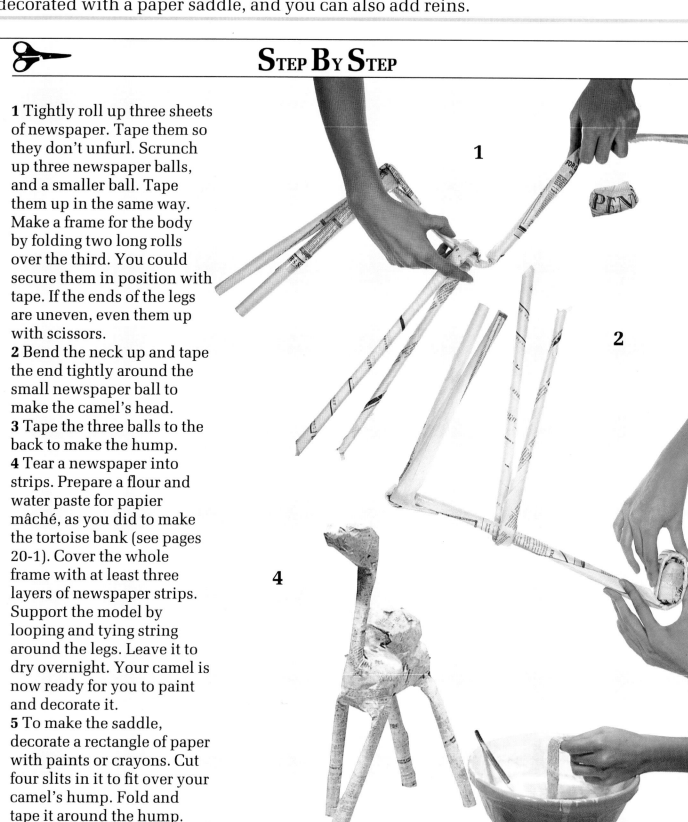

**YOU CAN USE:** tape string newspaper flour and water

**3**

**5**

Color the camel's body with bright poster paint. You could add paper ears, and paint on long eyelashes and a cranky expression. You could add reins and a tail of string, yarn, or cord.

You could decorate the saddle with sequins or glitter. You could also string saddlebags made with plastic cups across the saddle.

# Proud Peacock And Giraffe

The techniques described on the previous page can be used to make all kinds of animals. By changing the size of the body or the number of limbs, you can make a peacock, a giraffe, or any animal you choose.

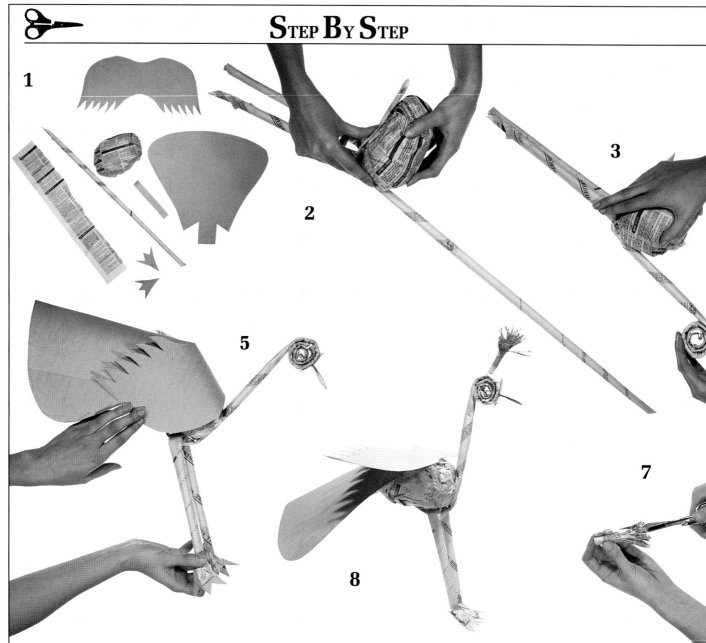

**1** To make the peacock, make a large newspaper ball and two long rolls. Cut cardboard shapes for the wings, feet and tail, using the patterns on pages 30-31.

**2** The peacock is similar to the swan on pages 22-23. Tape the longest roll around the body. Loop in the other roll for the legs.

**3** Curl the neck around a pencil to make the head. Fold and tape on a small cardboard strip for the beak.

**4** Fold and tape the tail around the body.

**5** Tape on the wings. Fold the legs over and then tape on the feet.

**6** To make the topknot, roll up a long, thin strip of newspaper.

**7** Cut a series of slits around one end. Unroll and reroll it, tape it together and tape it to the peacock's head.

string

tape

newspaper

cardboard

flour and water

**4**

This giraffe is made by following the steps on pages 24-25 for the camel. The giraffe has no hump, but a very long neck. You will need to roll up a short thin strip of newspaper for the horns.

Paint the giraffe's body yellow with brown patches. You could add a string or cord tail.

**6**

**8** Cover the frame with at least three layers of papier mâché. Tie string around the legs to support them while the model is drying. Leave it to dry overnight.

Paint on the peacock's gorgeous feathers and the "eyes" on its tail. You could also use sequins or glitter to decorate the tail.

# PRACTICAL TIPS

Below are a few practical hints that will help you with some of the projects described in this book.

## CREATING FLAPS

Use this tip for attaching the head and legs of your tortoise bank (see pages 20-21) and for fastening tube shapes onto your models.

Attaching a tube is easy if you use scissors to cut a number of short slits around one end of the tube first.

The slits form a series of flaps. Bend the flaps outward. Now you can press the tube flat onto the surface of your model. Use glue, tape, or papier mâché to attach the tube to the model.

## CUTTING A HOLE

This hint will help you make the pig for your farmyard mobile (see pages 8-9) and the base of your tortoise bank (pages 20-21). It is a useful technique whenever you need to make a hole in the middle of a piece of paper or cardboard, without cutting in from the edge. Place the paper shape that you want to cut out over a soft surface, such as an eraser.

Use a sharp pencil to pierce through the middle of your shape. You will now be able to insert the point of your scissors into the hole. Cut to the edge of the paper shape, and then cut around the shape with scissors.

## PAINTING

It may be difficult to get poster paint to stick to plastic. This tip will help.

Poster paint will stick to plastic if you squirt a little dishwashing liquid into your mixing water. Stir it around with your brush before you begin.

28

# MORE JUNK IDEAS

**PAPER:** comics and magazines, postcards and birthday cards, unused wallpaper, tissue.

The materials used most often in this book have been paper, cardboard and plastic packaging. Below are some more suggestions about the kinds of junk which can be used to make and decorate your models.

**WOOD:** spent matches, garden stakes, cotton spools, lollypop sticks.

**FABRIC:** yarn, socks, old clothes or sheets, cloth and felt scraps.

**PLASTIC:** food containers, candy and snack wrappers, buttons, broken toys.

**RUBBER:** rubber bands, balls, balloons, old rubber gloves.

**METAL:** soft drink cans, foil, springs, pipe cleaners, hangers, paper clips.

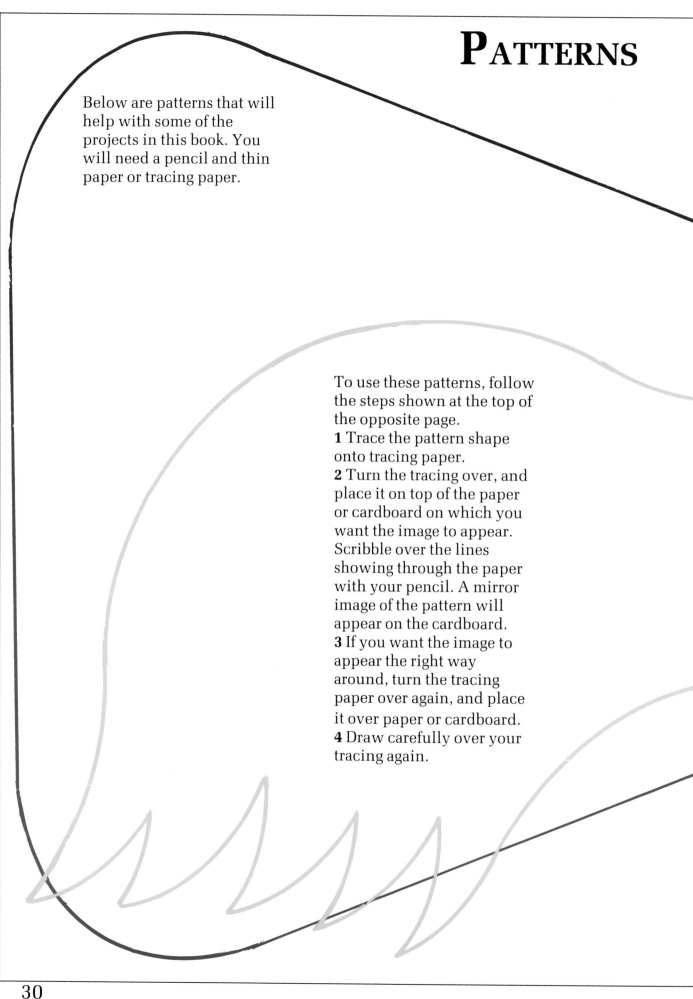

# PATTERNS

Below are patterns that will help with some of the projects in this book. You will need a pencil and thin paper or tracing paper.

To use these patterns, follow the steps shown at the top of the opposite page.
**1** Trace the pattern shape onto tracing paper.
**2** Turn the tracing over, and place it on top of the paper or cardboard on which you want the image to appear. Scribble over the lines showing through the paper with your pencil. A mirror image of the pattern will appear on the cardboard.
**3** If you want the image to appear the right way around, turn the tracing paper over again, and place it over paper or cardboard.
**4** Draw carefully over your tracing again.

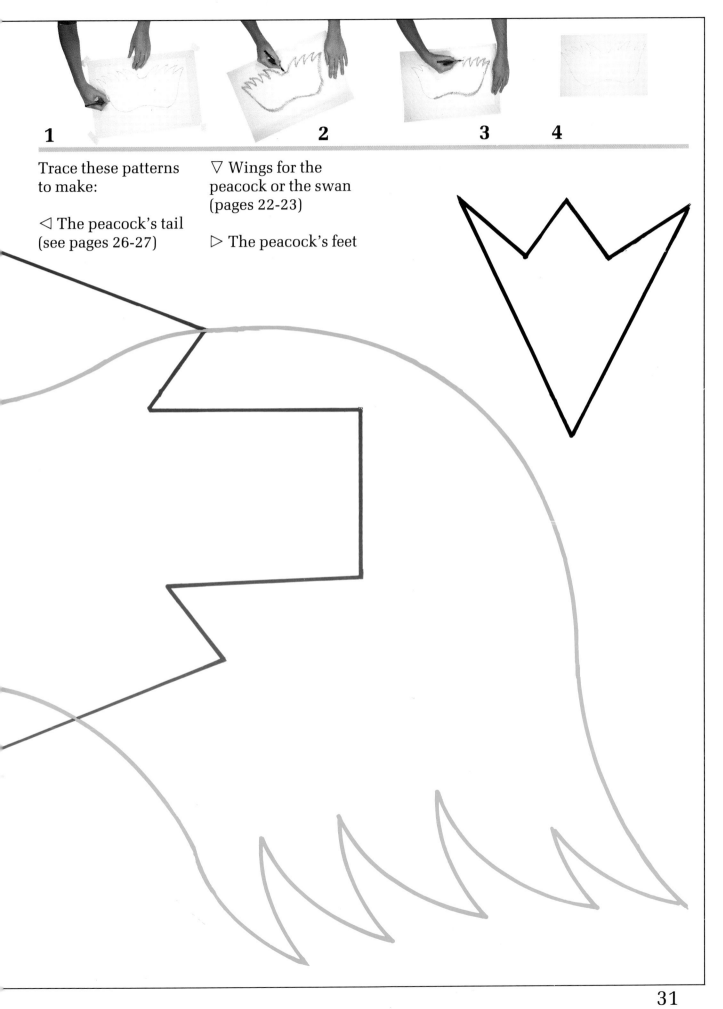

Trace these patterns
to make:

◁ The peacock's tail
(see pages 26-27)

▽ Wings for the
peacock or the swan
(pages 22-23)

▷ The peacock's feet

# INDEX

PRINTED IN BELGIUM BY
PROOST
INTERNATIONAL BOOK PRODUCTION